T0343965

Where Are the Animals?

by Frankie Ramirez

NATIONAL GEOGRAPHIC LEARNING | CENGAGE Learning

Many animals live here.

Where are the birds?

The birds are in the tree.

Where are the frogs?

The frogs are on the flower.

Where is the butterfly?

The butterfly is on the leaf.

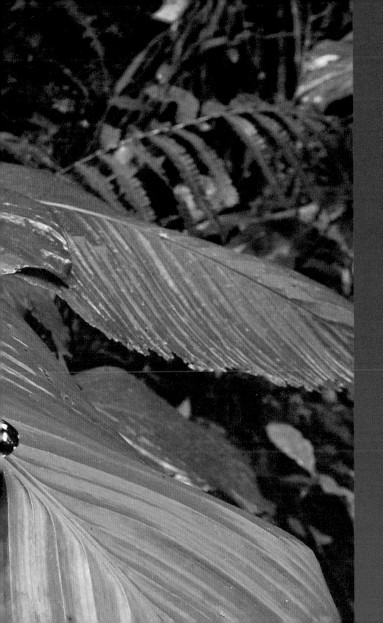

Where are all
the animals?

The animals are on the mountain.

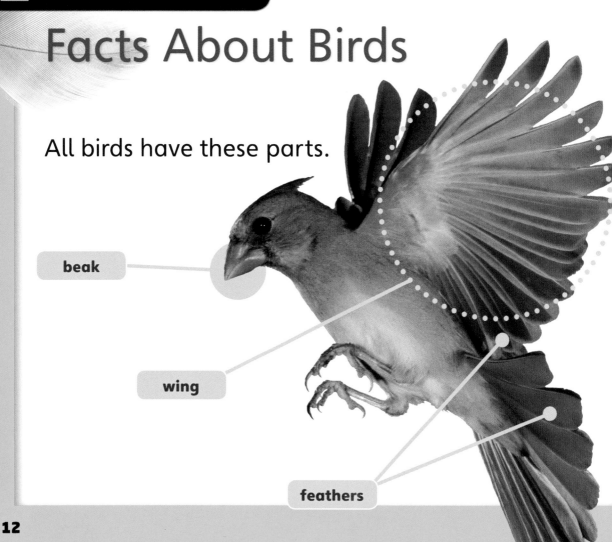

Facts About Birds

All birds have these parts.

beak

wing

feathers

All birds come from eggs.

hummingbird

This is a big bird.

ostrich

This is a little bird.

It comes from a little egg.

hummingbird eggs

ostrich egg

It comes from a big egg.

Fun with Nature

Find and circle the words for the pictures.

frog

bird

d	q	f	f
b	t	l	r
b	r	o	o
i	e	w	g
r	e	e	e
d	l	r	d

flower

tree

Color.

flower ▮   bird ▮

tree ▮   mountain ▮

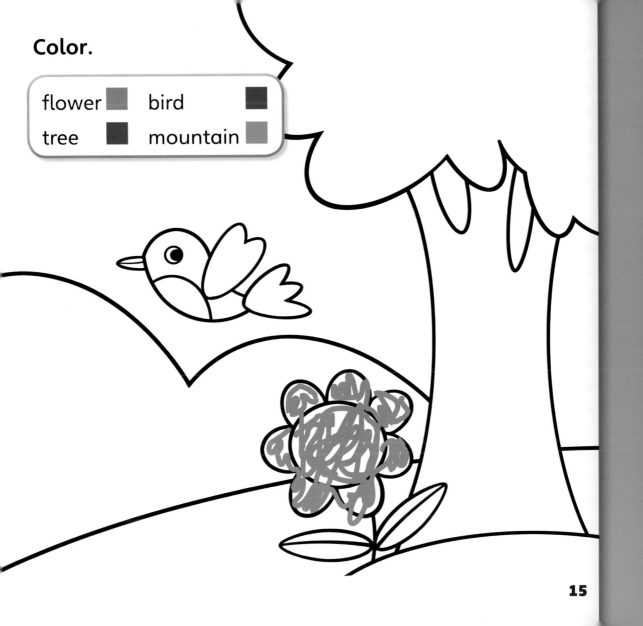

Glossary

butterfly

egg

leaf

parts